The
Persistence
of Faith

~~Scott Owens~~

Sandstone
Publishing

Grateful acknowledgment is due *Beloit Poetry Journal, Blue Unicorn, Charlotte Poetry Review, Cream City Review* and *Georgia Journal*, in which some of these poems were previously published.

PS
3565
.W5734
P47
1993
June 2002
ABN9361

Printed in the
United States of America
by Metro Printing
for
Sandstone Publishing
P.O. Box 36701
Charlotte, North Carolina 28236

First Edition

Cover photograph: Leslie Bivens

For Ann, Linda, and Shelley.
And most of all, for Karen.

"Comfort"

There is none
no immunity

no assurance of pardon
or prize.

There is denial
or the deliberate life

swearing off the daily news
like the fellow who

simply wouldn't round a corner
to see the world go up

the waves subside
the seas part

though there is
that lucky break

the brief caesura
of a random grace note:

the silver shiver of chimes
sounding a slow sweep of air

a ball lamp of cold spilled moon
. . .

- Shelley Crisp

For Ryan,

Whose leadership made
this wonderful night possible.

Scott Owen

10/6/94
Hickory

Contents

Between the Rails

He found God between two cars
of the Southern line from Greenwood to Clinton,
where his feet had frozen in place
on the small block holding the coupler.
His hand still held the ladder rung
he had swung down from
and could easily climb again
if only his feet would move.

He stood trembling between them,
watching the couplers push and pull
each other like locked jaws of dogs
fighting, watching the one hose
swell and breathe with the back
and forth pulling, the rough bed
shaking, the rocks pushing into the rails.

He heard the screaming of wheels
against rails, the pulsing at bolted
joints, the banging and groaning
of huge bodies against each other,
struggling it seemed
to come together or fall apart.

When he looked up he saw the face
twisted before him, the eyes
clenched shut, the mouth a perfect
O. He felt the breath hot
and loud around him, tasted
the sweat, smelled the odor
like wet leaves. The open mouth
screamed. The eyes flew open,
pierced him with anger, struck him

like a fist in his chest, taking
his breath away, holding him
tight against the back of the car.

The railroad people called his parents
from Clinton, and his father came to get him,
slapping him all the way home, shouting
about closed doors, groundings, railroads,
repeating never again, never again.
Afterwards it would always seem the same,
the hardened features, the stony eyes,
the fleeting images trapped between the rails,
the fist beating in his chest.

The Long Muscle of Life Takes the
Hard Way Out

It was only chaos of course because it wasn't his,
like any house you walk into and immediately want to change.
Like him it had always been there. And he had grown tired
of it touching him in its own way, turning out the lights
when he wasn't looking, flip-flopping heaven and earth
on a whim, constantly changing one thing to another.

He wanted to start from scratch, to recreate life
in his own image, lined, ruled, perfectly squared.
He wanted to make the universe like a diagram,
each thing pigeonholed neatly beneath another.

So finally with one atomic finger he levelled it all
into nothing, or rather into a mountain of glowing compost
he could dish out as he saw fit. He lay down a framework
of order, subjected night to day, earth to heaven,
everything to himself, made the sun as many times larger
than the moon as it was farther away from the earth.

"Believe," he told them, "that I am the one.
Follow my law and none other. Be happy
to have this purpose of praising what I am."

But at night, in the dark, it moved again the way it wanted,
slithered across the lines he'd made, became fruitful
and multiplied in all the wrong ways, flowed deeper in
and further out, left its gooey mess on his doorstep,
his window, on every wall he constructed.

So of course he grew tired of it again, tried to give it
one enormous bath to wash away the bits of life popping up
everywhere. But even before the waters receded it spun away,
danced on top of the waves, gathered enough silt to build
a mountain, grew lanterns to see beneath the murky deep.

So finally he said, "Fuck it. Here's a boy to play with.
Let him watch you for a while." And of course it consumed
the boy in no time, left him hanging cold on a tree,
and God, dejected and lost, retired, waiting
on the other side of darkness with his black book,
his fiery lake, an enormous chip on his shoulder.

The Imperfect Garden

There are things he never wanted this way,
things he never planned, the slip of hand
stretching the nose into elephant, flattening
the body into snake, the daydream winging
into nighthawk, the nightmare springing
to lion, his own sense of humor leading
to aardvark, manatee, pelican.

He thought that using his own body as model
he could do no wrong, but mistakes were made.
When he grew tired he lost his concentration.
Some were born deformed, others given bodies
too large or small, wings they couldn't use,
feet that only clung to tree or water.
Many were simply left unfinished.

He knew he could fix them, if he wanted,
make them just the way he sketched them out,
each one perfect and beautiful, but always
there was something in the way they walked,
talked, moved about without a backward glance,
without a care for him that made him say
this is life now, you can do nothing to stop it.

God, Creating the Birds, Envisions Adam
Detail from the North Porch of Chartres Cathedral

No feathers, no fins. Each thing he wanted
to outdo the last. How now could he
surpass these flowers of the air, his mind
already tired, his hands sore, his body
spent from shaping. Nothing less than himself
would do, he thought. His own image
in miniature, puppet, mannequin, mirror
that moves. Important now to forget the early
mistakes, jellyfish, plankton, platypus,
to focus on this final act of creation.

In the darkness he saved from his own
restless hands he drank the wine he created,
his only company the quiet angels of his mind.
He will have no wings. That night he slept
the troubled sleep of dreams. He saw faces
that mocked his own, fingers that picked
his skin apart, mouths that spat in the hands
that made them. *His teeth will be like white
soldiers, angry and hard.*

Early the next day, his eyes barely open,
his head still humming from the night before,
he scraped the flesh from his own face,
opened a mouth, pressed his thumb hard
into the wells of eyes, pulled up ears
and nose, stretched out torso, arms, legs,
fingers, toes. He worked for hours shaping
the supple curve of back, rounding the buttocks,
pinching the tight cup of prick and balls.
His hands will be like these, clumsy and precise.

At last he draped it over the white sticks
he cherished, dredged the life again
from his lungs, spat it into the mouth,
called it man, son of God, keeper of earth,
dropped it headfirst, naked, crying,
bruised and bloody to the ground.

The Fifth Day

On the first day there was only
the sound of his own making,
a noise as quiet as thought.
On the second day he heard for the first
time the earth cracking with heat,
the water moving against itself,
the wheels of the sky spinning,
and the long silence beside him.
On the third day he heard the sun
unfolding a flower, heard the vines
creeping across the earth,
leaves stretching outward,
wind shaking limbs together.

Yesterday sang all night
in his ears, warbled like light
across his mind, rattled his eyes
open, touched his lips,
still without sound.

Today there is speaking,
there is crying,
there is howling at the moon
he threw out like a spare part,
there are the many-voweled voices
of animals calling each other by name.

Tomorrow he will learn
what his own tongue could do
if he would let it,
if he would give himself
just one person to talk to,
one person to talk to him
without saying yessir,
nosir, amen.

Learning the Names

Imagine Adam discovering the names
of every living thing for the first
time, calling out the names of every
beast in the field, calling the red
leaves maple, the ever green pine,
calling out bergamot and burdock,
waxwing and shrike, iris and owl
without reason or rhyme but just
the joy of weight on his tongue.

Imagine Noah calling them
into his ark by twos, renaming
the ones he never knew, calling
the horned ones rhino, the long
bird anhinga, the bright snake coral,
the one that never moves mantis.

Imagine naming things the first
time, releasing the roll of vowels
in your mouth, spitting out sounds
your body knew before you.
Imagine later discovering consonants,
the hum in your throat with your mouth
closed, the small explosions when
you open it, the different winds
blowing before your face.

Then you renamed things, better,
but still without right or wrong,
discovering the well-made words
that framed in mouth's shape
what the hands held, the perfect
names of things like breast, song, yes.

Why Angels Are Always Fat

He took all my pretty ones with him,
the ones with tight bellies, long
streaming hair, faces thin as blades,
the ones who had fallen in love
with themselves, and had reason to do so.
He left me only these soft and silent
mounds of flesh, these uninspired,
these bodies needing wings twice
the size you've imagined.

He took all my hungry ones with him,
the ones with tiger breath wanting
to get ahead, the ones who ate meat,
drank fire, howled at the moon.
He left me not with shepherds
but sheep fattening on sugar
and sweets, their wrinkled bodies
growing chins instead of desire.

When I clapped my hands the pretty ones
came slow, always touching themselves
below the waist, lingering to see
how this and then that felt against them.
He never clapped at all, just kept
his body covered in mirrors
so they'd follow him anywhere.

Of course I had to let him go.
That was no way to run a heaven,
everyone looking at him,
myself no longer the center of thought.
But now when I clap no one comes
at all, not that I wish they would.

Those he left stuff themselves
on dumplings and cream, their bodies
turning to clouds heavy with rain.

Sometimes when he leaves his lights on
I like to watch them from my dark chair.
I like to see the shapes they make
with each other, see their bodies burn
with forbidden fire, see what they remember,
see my face reflected there.

Remembering Walking

That was before God came down
and dropped his half-baked figures
in the garden, before Adam and Eve
were evicted for knowing how perfect
the shape of snake and grass go together.
That was when the miles were shorter,
the hills easier to climb,
when I could listen to my feet
scratching through dry grass, stamping
wet rocks, tramping the earth,
when I still worried about stones
lodging in the pink pads of my toes.

I remember walking
and do not miss it.
No one else hugs the earth
like I do,
wrapping body and soul around
the quiet curve of land. No one else
knows the measure of every grain
of sand they pass over. No one else
can know the scaly skin of pines,
the twisted burl of oak, the slick
puddle of plums changing into earth
like brothers.

Veronica's Veil

It was his face I wanted to save,
to love into this dull rag, press
to my cheek, wipe clean of dust, sweat,
tears. There was nothing holy in my desire
to have some shade of perfection
for my own, to hold the strong nose,
the full lips, the hard, fine features
of a man in the cup of my own hands.

You were there. You saw how perfect
he was, the sores ripe and wet
as bruised fruit, the veins running
like roots beneath his skin.
This face deserved no worms
to consume it, no black hole
of earth to conceal it, no dark
future of creeping up through veins
of lilies, rolling like spitballs
in the intestines of worms, dangling
through fetid waters in rats' teeth.

Look at your own face. Feel the dark
seeds of your eyes, the bright
bulbs of cheek and chin, the stem
of your nose, your lips' soft
petals, stamen teeth, pistil tongue.
Nothing this beautiful, this gentle,
should be torn limb from limb,
should face death on this earth,
bleed in these hands able to save it
only as a leaf dried between two pages.

How to See a Crucifix
After Salvador Dalí's **Christ of St. John of the Cross**

The arm's shadow drawn longer,
thinner than any arm could be.
The hands like a piano master,
a magician poised to strike
his trick of resurrection,
like some unformed wings unable
to fly. The head down, the sense
of hanging off the cross,
unable to resist a simple
law of gravity. Even this neck
bowed beneath heaven's oppression.

This could be Galilee or Lake Norman.
It would be difficult to hang this way
in any place that wasn't home.

All the things that weren't
supposed to happen already have.
A woman who never fell from grace
had grace fall on her. A child
was spared. A man who forgave
everything was unforgiven.

Why should it be seen as something
perfect? Holy rapture of resurrection.
Smile of understanding. Perfect
cross of body unaffected, arms
unwrenched, shoulders untwisted.
Flaccid dream of salvation.

You think too much of your life
to want it this way, to think
this I could bear, to want
to be untouched by the strength
of an arm twisted alive in pain,
a body bent beyond recognition,
beyond the sign of its own name.

Saint Sebastian's Widow

"A pious widow found him and nursed him back to health"
— Lives of the Saints

Pierced with arrows and left for dead,
I found you hanging by your hands
from a knotted oak, your head pitched
forward, your face hidden beneath
the wet rag of your hair. I was old,
had been alone too long, had forgotten
how beautiful a man's chest could be,
the soft thatch of hair, the small-boned
ribs pressing against the flesh,
curving around the heart. Even stretched
to snapping and streaked with blood,
I wanted to cup my hands around
your breasts' unopened buds, lay my head
in the pale hollow of your chest,
rise and fall with your breathing.

I cut you down, broke off the arrows,
and struggled to carry you home,
not caring who saw me, what names
they called me. Once there I laid you
in my only bed, dug out the heads,
slowly, like pulling weeds, careful
to displace as little flesh as necessary,
sponging up the blood and packing
the wounds with my softest cloth.

For day your eyes stayed closed, your head
lolling to one side, your chest
barely moving. I dripped water
and broth slowly into your mouth.
I offered your body flowers and perfumes,

washed it daily with the best soaps
I could find, lingering over your soft
skin, the limp stem of your loins,
gently fingering each pale curve
of muscle, each long ridge of bone.
At night when you moaned with pain, I rushed
to your side. I watched your back swell
with air, held your face in my hands,
ran my fingers through your hair.
I wanted to lick the sweat from your brow,
suck the chill from your spine.

I nursed you back to consciousness,
kept you through your weakness,
fed you soup and bones and whatever
meat I could find, and you saying
nothing anyday but "Bless you."
When you started caring for yourself
again, I helped however I could,
enjoying the weight of your body on mine,
your arm thrown across my shoulders,
your hand holding tightly to mine.

On the first day you left the house,
you walked back to where I found you
and started preaching again.
A crowd gathered, first the people,
then the soldiers. I watched you
from below, your face filling with glory,
your hands waving through the air,
your chest swelling beneath the robe
I made you. I barely understood
your words, but the soldiers knew you,
taunted you, spat at you,
called you ghost, deadman, Christian.

When you turned and swore at them,
condemned them, I saw the anger rise
in their faces. I saw them moving towards you.
I saw how you continued shouting words
like God, resurrection, salvation.
I wanted to save you, to carry you home
again, to tell them you didn't mean it,
you were mad with sickness, but I knew
nothing I could do would stop you or them.

I watched them beat you with clubs till your body
was broken, your face bloated with bruises,
your chest splattered, not streaked, with blood.
I watched them and cried to see your head
give way, your chest give way,
your beauty falling off in pieces.
I watched them finally toss you in the gutter,
a limp rag staining the water.
I left you there for someone else
to bury, to chase the rats away,
to clean your body, throw dirt
over what was once so white.
I could not save you again.
I would not hold your ruined body,
cry in your dead hair.

The Right One

Suddenly, there was the right one.
Where there had been confusion,
now the choice was clear.
Everyone knew it was the right one
because it said so.

Men cried. Women swooned.
Children did what children do
singing songs about the right one.

Almost at once there were right one t-shirts
and hats, right one shoes and jackets.
There were bumper stickers that said
The Right One Saves; The Right One
Is Lord; The Right One Is My Co-Pilot.

Before long there were right one cults
in every country. Monks in Tibet
chanted hymns about the right one.
The great tribes of Africa danced
around the right one's shining altar.
The Russians welcomed the right one
with open arms. All the great poets
wrote great poems called The Right One.

Eventually the right one was all
that mattered. People gave their lives
to the right one, knowing the right one
could save the world. They made it their
mission to bring the right one to those
who didn't have it. Governments ruled
by the words of the right one.
Those opposed to the right one

were strung up, crucified, chased
from one town to another.

Those who remained tried everything
to be like the right one.
They stripped themselves bare,
ran naked through the streets.
They abstained from everything
except the right one. They tore
their flesh. They fasted.
They sacrificed themselves
until at last there was only one,
the right one.

The Persistence of Doubt

I want to say there's a reason the hawk's tail
is the same red as pine needles in November.
I want to say his hornet's nest body in bare trees
means that someone is watching.

I want to say the kingfisher's blue splashing back
    to water
shows how everything returns to what it came from.
I want to say the brown fingers of rivers wrapping
    around everything I know
shows that something holds us close to the earth
    we're born to.
I want to say that blackbirds streaming out of treetops
proves that heaven and earth share the same ways
    of turning.

But the wind rushes by me like a voice heard through
    a wall,
a lesson whose meaning can never be clear.

And the past gathers behind me like nightfall
and the night grows wider
with every mile
with every minute gone by
and the distance between me
and where I was
and the place I want to be
and tomorrow

and tomorrow
—I can't imagine what it will be like—
and tomorrow
—I will let go of it today—
and tomorrow
—how could you hold such a thing on your tongue?

25

The Persistence of Faith

Some things he knows are true,
the sound of rain rising, then falling,
heavy, then lighter, on the roof,
on the steps outside, the light
of the Christmas star swinging
in the doorway, in the wind,
the shapes of cars sliding down
lit streets in the night, the lights
of windows left on for someone
not sleeping, someone not there.

Some things he can only imagine,
the wind, the leaves like footsteps
at the door, the limbs brushing the sky's
dust of clouds, the drivers
of cars almost lost in the night,
in the rain, the destinations,
the faces waiting in the windows,
the stars like the eyes of God.

The Arrival of Wings

The wings come first—
great fins rising out of your back.
It'll happen when you're alone,
in the hospital room, beneath
the water, your hand busy in bed.

Trying them on, you'll soar
into walls, tangles of trees,
do-si-do in the air, nosedive
to the ground, beat a circle
of bruises about your head.

You'll remark how unlike
the little fat ones you feel.
You'll wonder how they
in their pudge and ignorance
could manage their own so well.

They're just too big, really,
and too new. They could enclose you,
if you knew how. They could
lift you to the sky, if you
could find some suitable rhythm,

could tame your great flapping,
control your flailing about.
As it is, they only tire you,
lash welts on your back,
beat you half to death.

A Lake, A Leaf, the Bud, A Grave

*"Slowly, very slowly, they emerge out of the flower-pot
of the body"*

> — Katherina Anghelaki-Rooke
> Trans. by Kimon Friar

It starts with your hand floating on water,
your feet leaving no wet spots on the floor.
She was surprised to find how easily she stayed
on top, feeling weightless even on the thin skin
of lake. When she stood up she had to be careful
not to be seen. It's not walking on water exactly
but floating just above the surface of everything.

Waking in the middle of the night you move
to the mirror and find your entire face
dilated, a chicken's eye untrusting flight.
You barely remember what you've seen,
and even this is enough to keep you from sleep.

Already her body yearns for earth,
her feet linger over roots, her hands
try to fly away like leaves, her mouth
leans to kiss every flower she sees.

One day you think you see yourself
disappearing in sunlight, your body scattered
like dust. You move quickly towards shadows.
The strange hair in your back begins to feel
like a feather, your feet curl like talons.
You know now and tell people not to worry.

When she tries to speak, her mouth
only circles figures of light and air.
She watches them float into the sky like stars,
blurred, uncertain, disappearing into darkness.

Reaching out to the people she loves
she feels nothing but the light around them.
She no longer knows the imperfections of face,
hand, breast. If she could shed this skin
her body would burst into flight,
her wings cut the sky like sharp
limbs tossed erratic in wind.

Looking for Faces in the Night Sky

These are things anyone could have made
up. The stars are nothing but stars,
and playing dot-to-dot in the night
sky makes anything possible.
Years ago from the stone porch
my grandfather pointed them out:
the lion, the great bear, the hunter's sword.
This one he called Mary and showed me
how the stars made a woman's face.

Looking for faces in the night sky
we string stars into shapes of things
we fear or long to remember.
I see spider, sparrowhawk, bobwhite.
This one I'll call woman becoming
an angel, the grotesque buds of wings
sprouting in her back.

The Angel's Search for Heaven on Earth

In the morning he returns to heaven,
dragging his wings behind him,
his halo loose around his ears.

The night is a bad taste in his mouth,
a memory of retching on doorsteps,
passing out feathers in a bar.

He remembers losing at darts and quarters,
trading small miracles for beer,
swallowing goldfish on a dare.

He remembers tattoos, a rose
on a man's chest, a tiny cross
between his eyes, the pricks in his own

skin. He remembers the taste of sweat
and cigarettes, flaming shots of rum.
He remembers dancing with a girl

named Sylvia, feeling the pink
swelling against his chest, touching flesh
he'd nearly forgotten. He remembers walking

in the moon's erotic O, her hands
on his ass, stroking his wings.
He remembers dripping cold water

on her chest, watching the skin shrink,
then glisten, stretch, warm to falling.
He remembers her body beside him,

her face a pool of sunshine,
her feet painted with raindrops,
crescent moons, starry nights.

He wonders how the world could help
but hold such life, how things like this
are let to fade, pass away.

He can't help but wonder how much
faith he has spread today, how there
could be any wrong in this quiet
touching some small piece of heaven.

In the Cathedral of Fallen Trees

Each time he thinks something
special will happen; he'll see
the sky resting on bent backs
of limbs; he'll find the wind
hiding in hands of leaves;
he'll read between the lines
of some tree just fallen.

Because he found that trees were not
forever, that even trees he knew
grew recklessly towards falling,
he gave in to wisteria's plan
to glorify the dead. He sat down
beneath the arches of limbs reaching
above him, felt the light spread
through stained glass windows of leaves.

He did not expect the hawk to be here.
He had no design to find the meaning
of wild ginger, to see leaves soaked
with slime trails of things just past.

He thought only to listen
to the persistent breathing of trees,
to quiet whispers of leaves in wind.

Each time he thinks something
special will happen; he returns
with a handful of dirt, a stone
shaped a bowl, a small tree
growing rootbound against a larger.

Mother Which Art

Mother, who made me?

Why, I did, my child.

How, mother?

Out of my own flesh and blood I made you.
I fed you the food of my own body,
gave you the milk of my breast,
the bread of my mouth,
the water of all I took in,
loved you towards your first breath,
carried you like the part of me you will always be.

Where, mother? Where did you make me?

Here, inside me. You lay inside me
until roses bloomed in your cheeks.
You moved like a leaf unfurling, stretching
your arms and legs, opening yourself
to all the light I offered,
then opening my own soft petals
to wake to both our crying.

Make another, like me, another child from inside you.

No, child. For that I would need to make a father first.

Who mother? Who was my father?

A god, a force of nature, a demon
of my own creation, of my own mind's
needing, a swan, a bull, a spirit
from heaven, a serpent, a flea,
a crow, a wolf, a bear,
a mirror with your face,
almost anything I want him to be.

Common Ground

My brother has never kept a single lake,
a single lost grave to himself.
Always he calls, then waits till I
can come, lets me lead the way,
find it like the first time,
shouting the names I know, the shapes
of bird and stone, tree and fish.

Once in the same day I saw a kestrel,
a mantis, an arrowhead and took it
as a sign, though since I have seen
each in their own days
and miles away from each other.

I do not believe God will bend to kiss
this mouth. I do not believe the wine
will turn. But something knows the moment
of sunflower, the time of crow's open wing,
the time of moss growing on rock,
and water washing it away.

This is the faith I've wanted, to know
that even now we are capable of such
sacrifice, such willingness to love.

About Scott Owens . . .

Scott Owens is originally from Greenwood, SC. He has attended Ohio University, the University of North Carolina at Charlotte, and the University of North Carolina at Greensboro, and worked in a tobacco field, a cotton mill, a nursing home, and a hardware store, among other places. He currently lives in Charlotte, NC, teaches at the University of North Carolina at Greensboro, and serves as Associate Editor of the *Southern Poetry Review*. He has also served as Assistant Editor of *Sanskrit* and *Genesis*, and as chairperson of Seon, the Arts Alliance, and has conducted creativity workshops at the high school and college levels. He has received awards in poetry from the Academy of American Poets and the North Carolina Writers Network. His poems have appeared in numerous journals, including *Cream City Review, Cottonwood, Cimarron Review, Beloit Poetry Journal, Laurel Review, Greensboro Review, Iron* (England), *Poet & Critic, Sun Dog, Pembroke, Crucible,* and *Charlotte Poetry Review. The Persistence of Faith* is his first collection of poems.